BILLIE JEAN KING AND THE BATTLE OF THE SEXES

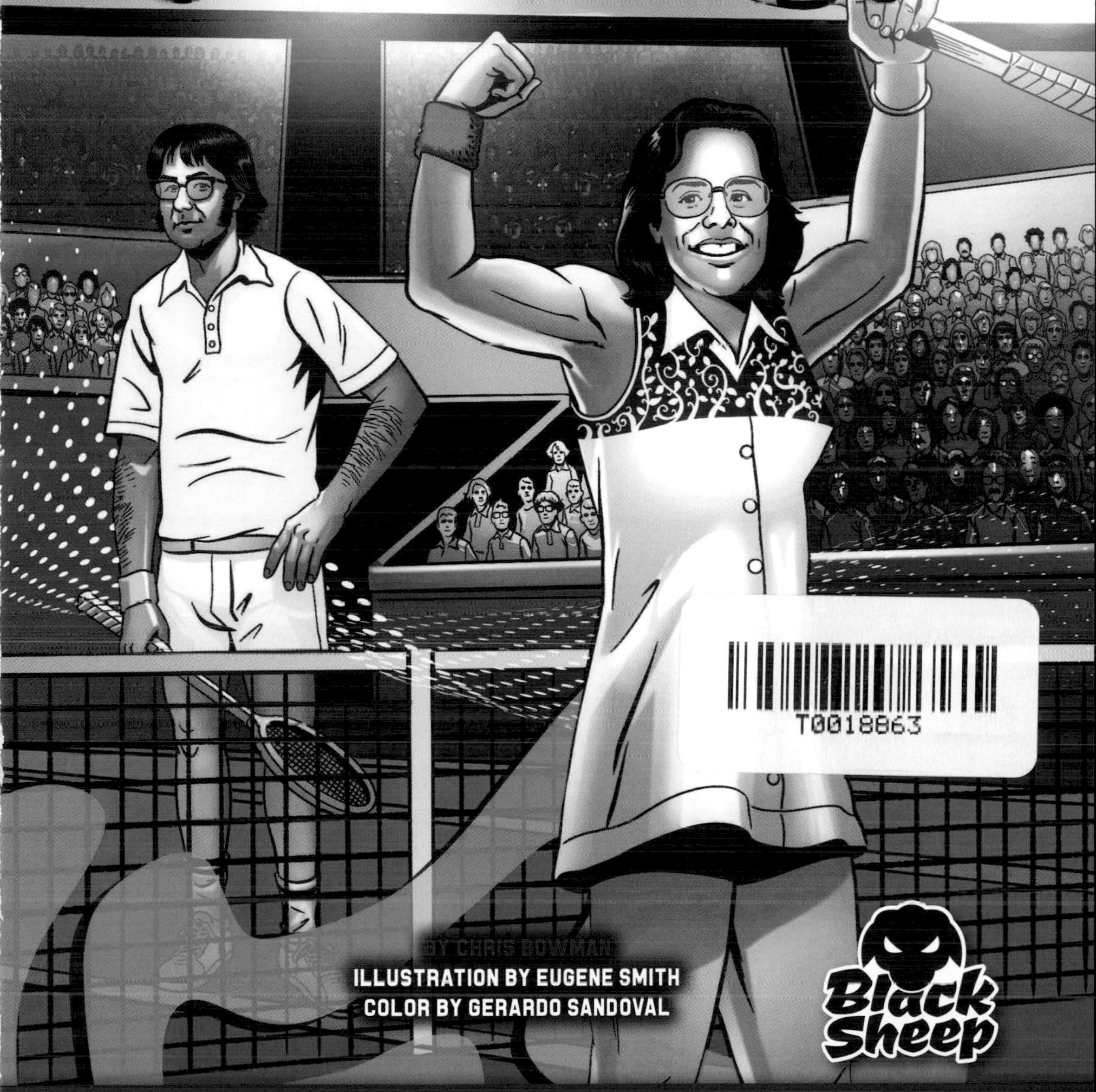

BY CHRIS BOWMAN
ILLUSTRATION BY EUGENE SMITH
COLOR BY GERARDO SANDOVAL

BELLWETHER MEDIA • MINNEAPOLIS, MN

STRAY FROM REGULAR READS
WITH BLACK SHEEP BOOKS.
FEEL A RUSH WITH EVERY READ!

This edition first published in 2024 by Bellwether Media, Inc.

No part of this publication may be reproduced in whole or in part without written permission of the publisher.
For information regarding permission, write to Bellwether Media, Inc., Attention: Permissions Department,
6012 Blue Circle Drive, Minnetonka, MN 55343.

Library of Congress Cataloging-in-Publication Data

Names: Bowman, Chris, 1990- author. | Smith, Eugene (Illustrator), illustrator.
Title: Billie Jean King and the battle of the sexes / by Chris Bowman ; [illustrated by Eugene Smith].
Description: Minneapolis, MN : Bellwether Media, Inc., 2024. | Series: Black sheep. Greatest moments in sports |
    Includes bibliographical references and index. | Audience: Ages 7-13 years | Audience: Grades 4-6 | Summary:
    "Exciting illustrations follow the events of Billie Jean King playing the Battle of the Sexes. The combination of brightly
    colored panels and leveled text is intended for students in grades 3 through 8"– Provided by publisher.
Identifiers: LCCN 2023017797 (print) | LCCN 2023017798 (ebook) | ISBN 9798886875065 (library binding) |
    ISBN 9798886875560 (paperback) | ISBN 9798886876949 (ebook)
Subjects: LCSH: King, Billie Jean–Juvenile literature. | Riggs, Bobby, 1918-1995–Juvenile literature. | Tennis players–
    United States–Biography–Juvenile literature. | Tennis–Tournaments–History–20th century–Juvenile literature. |
    Sex discrimination in sports–United States–Juvenile literature. | Sports–Sex differences–Juvenile literature. | Women
    athletes–United States–Social conditions–Juvenile literature. | Sports rivalries–United States–History–Juvenile literature.
Classification: LCC GV994.A1 B68 2024 (print) | LCC GV994.A1 (ebook) | DDC 796.342092/2–dc23/eng/20230518
LC record available at https://lccn.loc.gov/2023017797
LC ebook record available at https://lccn.loc.gov/2023017798

Editor: Betsy Rathburn   Designer: Andrea Schneider

Printed in the United States of America, North Mankato, MN.

TABLE OF CONTENTS

Red text identifies historical quotes.

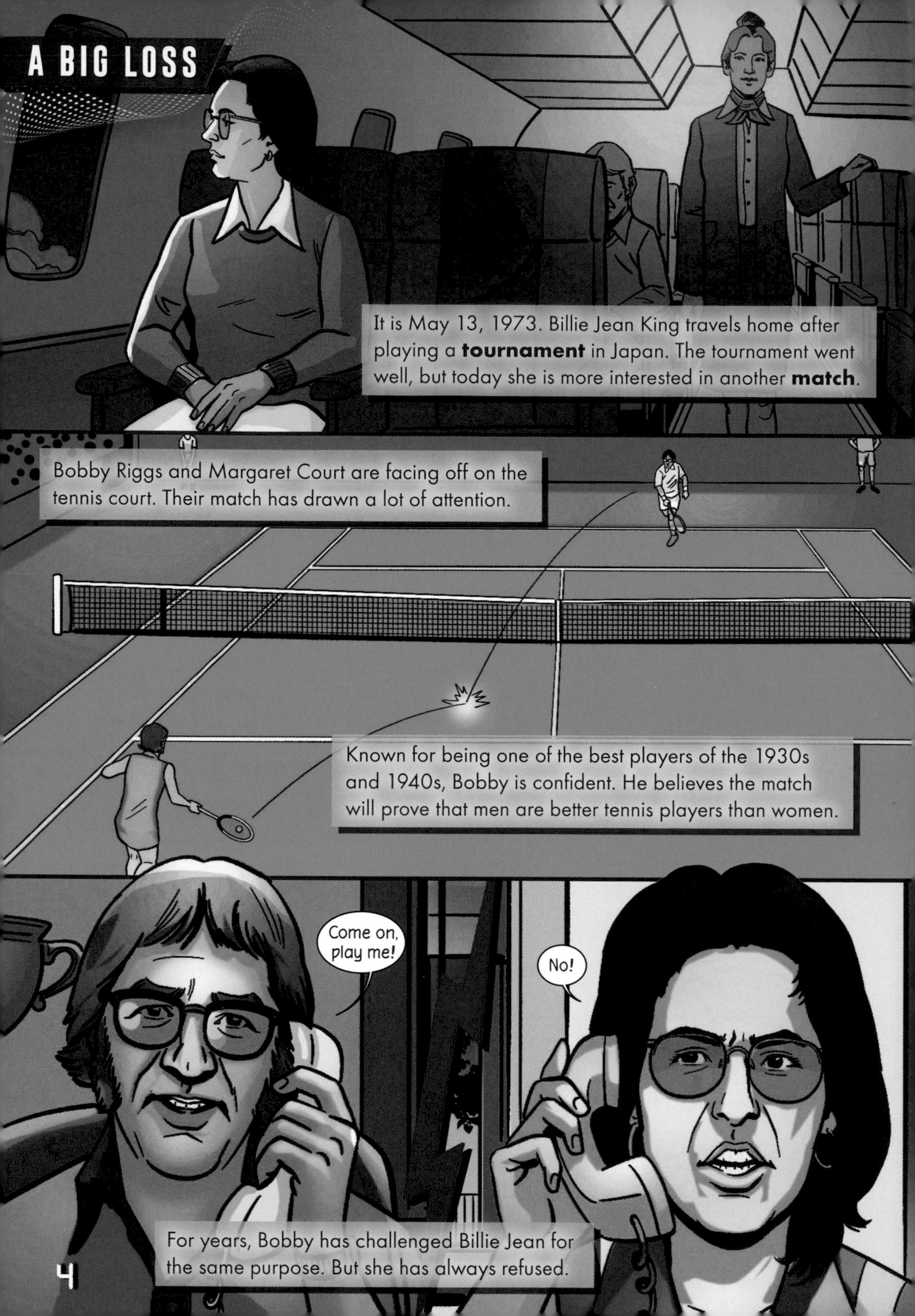
A BIG LOSS
It is May 13, 1973. Billie Jean King travels home after playing a **tournament** in Japan. The tournament went well, but today she is more interested in another **match**.
Bobby Riggs and Margaret Court are facing off on the tennis court. Their match has drawn a lot of attention.
Known for being one of the best players of the 1930s and 1940s, Bobby is confident. He believes the match will prove that men are better tennis players than women.
Come on, play me!
No!
For years, Bobby has challenged Billie Jean for the same purpose. But she has always refused.

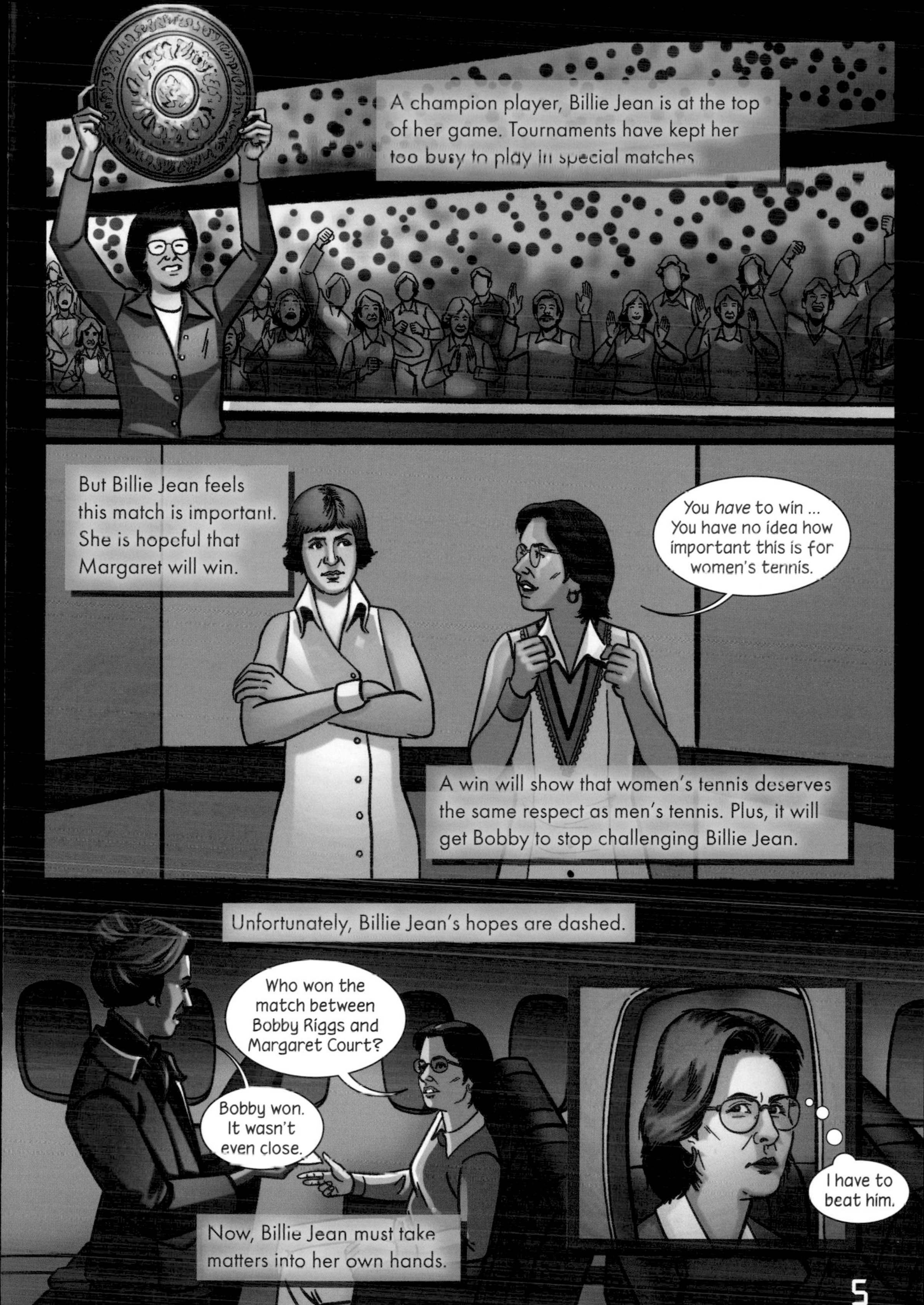
A champion player, Billie Jean is at the top of her game. Tournaments have kept her too busy to play in special matches.
But Billie Jean feels this match is important. She is hopeful that Margaret will win.
You *have* to win ... You have no idea how important this is for women's tennis.
A win will show that women's tennis deserves the same respect as men's tennis. Plus, it will get Bobby to stop challenging Billie Jean.
Unfortunately, Billie Jean's hopes are dashed.
Who won the match between Bobby Riggs and Margaret Court?
Bobby won. It wasn't even close.
I have to beat him.
Now, Billie Jean must take matters into her own hands.

BECOMING THE BEST

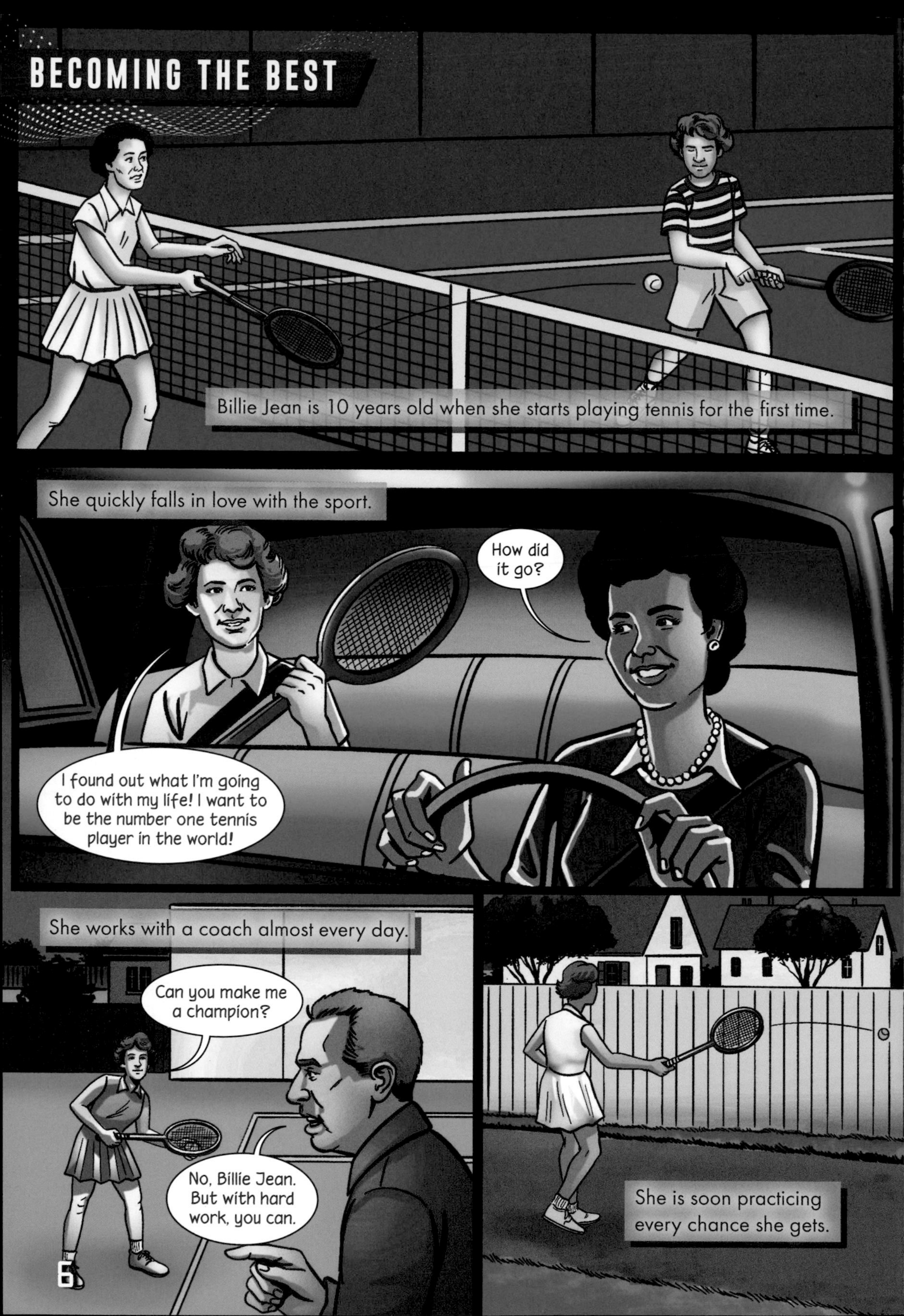

Billie Jean is 10 years old when she starts playing tennis for the first time.
She quickly falls in love with the sport.
How did it go?
I found out what I'm going to do with my life! I want to be the number one tennis player in the world!
She works with a coach almost every day.
Can you make me a champion?
No, Billie Jean. But with hard work, you can.
She is soon practicing every chance she gets.

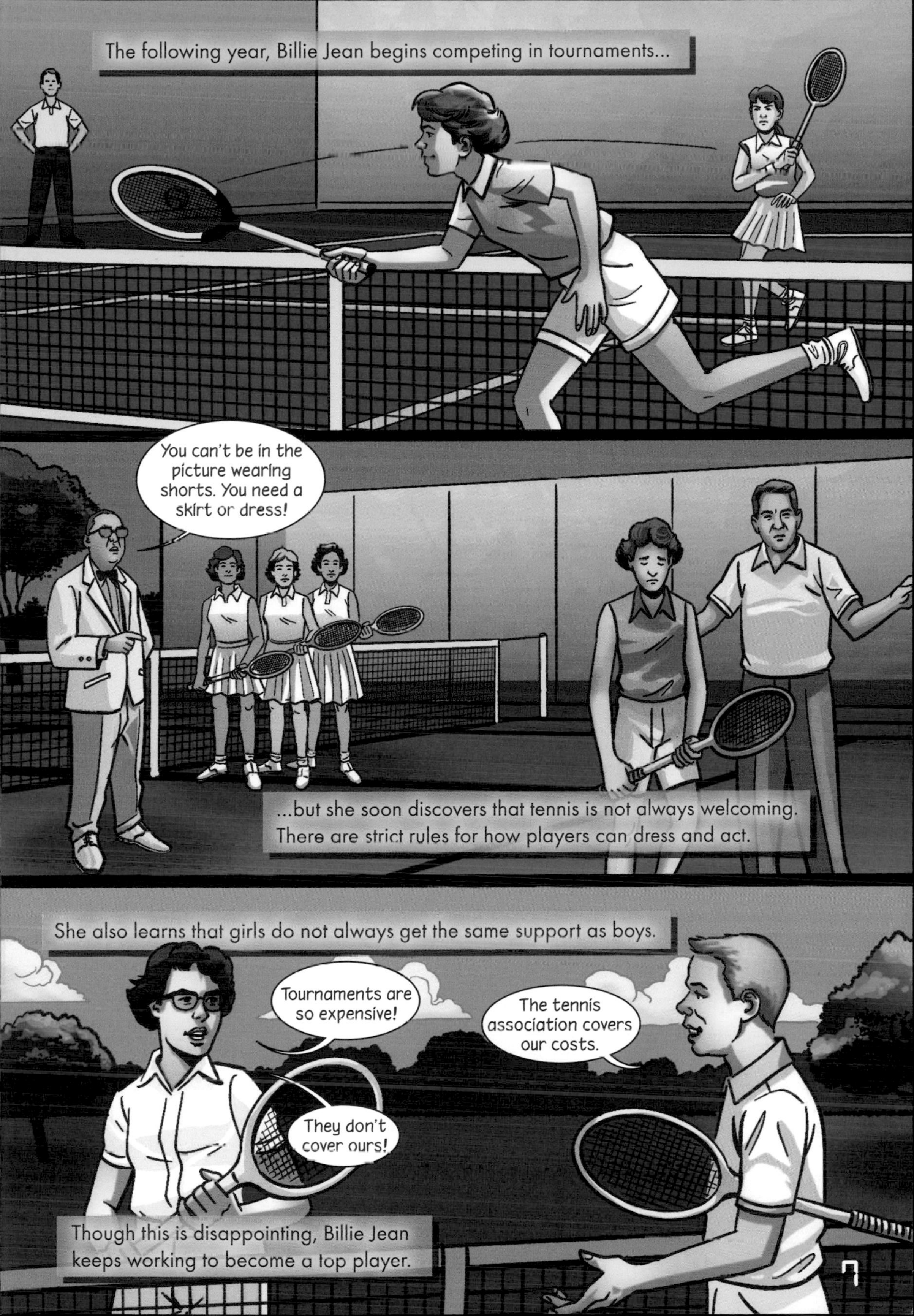
The following year, Billie Jean begins competing in tournaments...
You can't be in the picture wearing shorts. You need a skirt or dress!
...but she soon discovers that tennis is not always welcoming. There are strict rules for how players can dress and act.
She also learns that girls do not always get the same support as boys.
Tournaments are so expensive!
The tennis association covers our costs.
They don't cover ours!
Though this is disappointing, Billie Jean keeps working to become a top player.

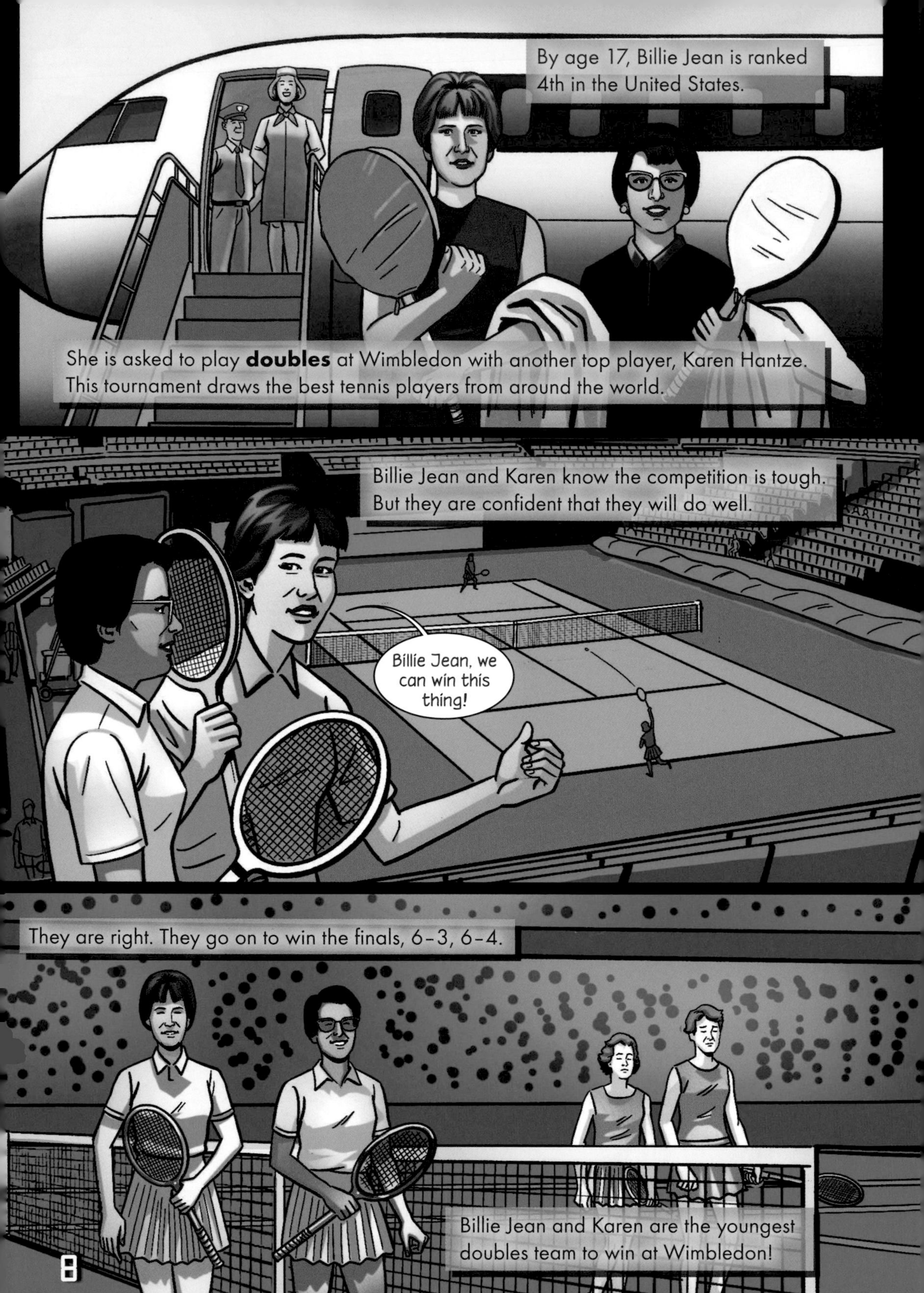
By age 17, Billie Jean is ranked 4th in the United States.
She is asked to play **doubles** at Wimbledon with another top player, Karen Hantze. This tournament draws the best tennis players from around the world.
Billie Jean and Karen know the competition is tough. But they are confident that they will do well.
Billie Jean, we can win this thing!
They are right. They go on to win the finals, 6–3, 6–4.
Billie Jean and Karen are the youngest doubles team to win at Wimbledon!

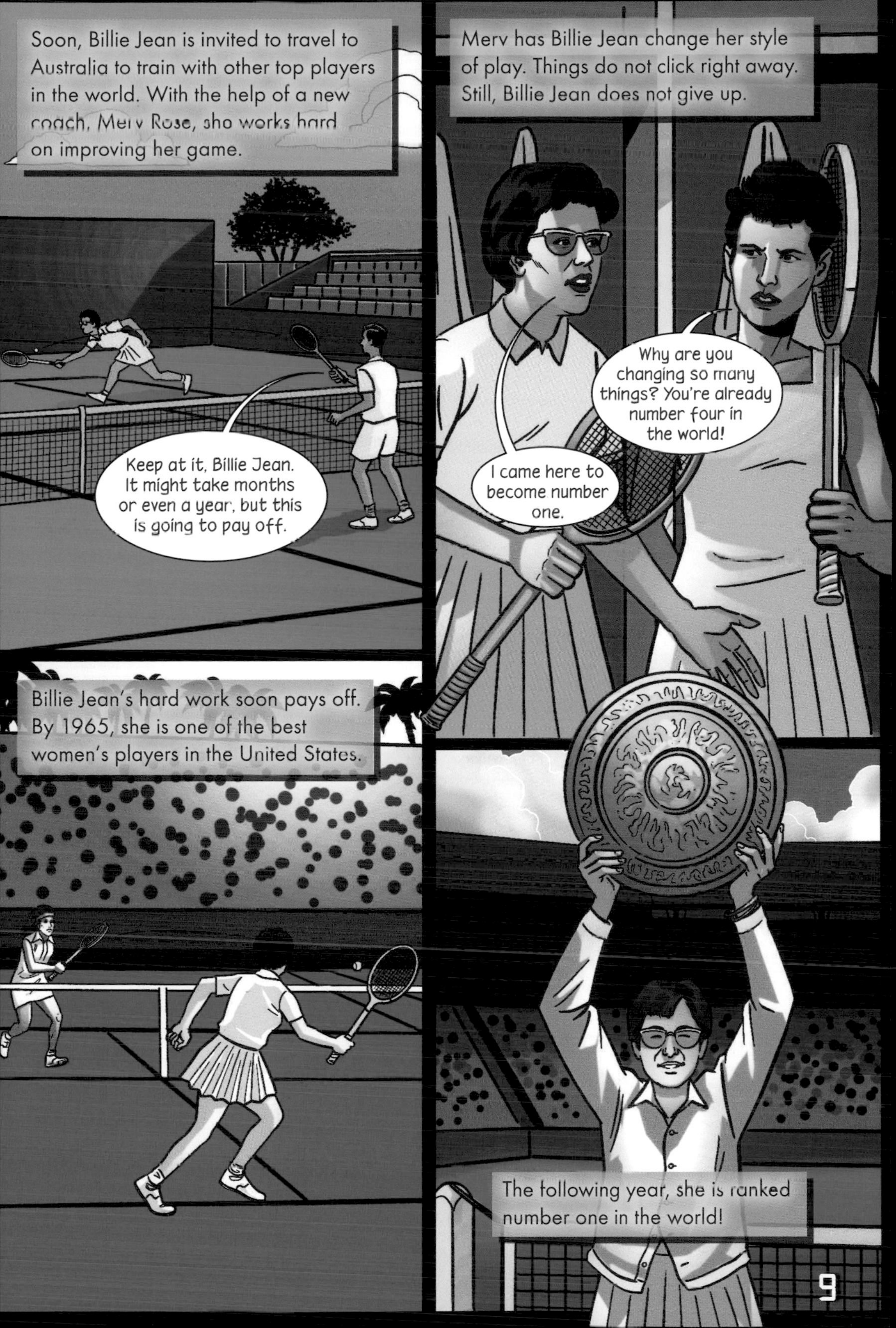
Soon, Billie Jean is invited to travel to Australia to train with other top players in the world. With the help of a new coach, Merv Rose, she works hard on improving her game.
Keep at it, Billie Jean. It might take months or even a year, but this is going to pay off.
Merv has Billie Jean change her style of play. Things do not click right away. Still, Billie Jean does not give up.
Why are you changing so many things? You're already number four in the world!
I came here to become number one.
Billie Jean's hard work soon pays off. By 1965, she is one of the best women's players in the United States.
The following year, she is ranked number one in the world!

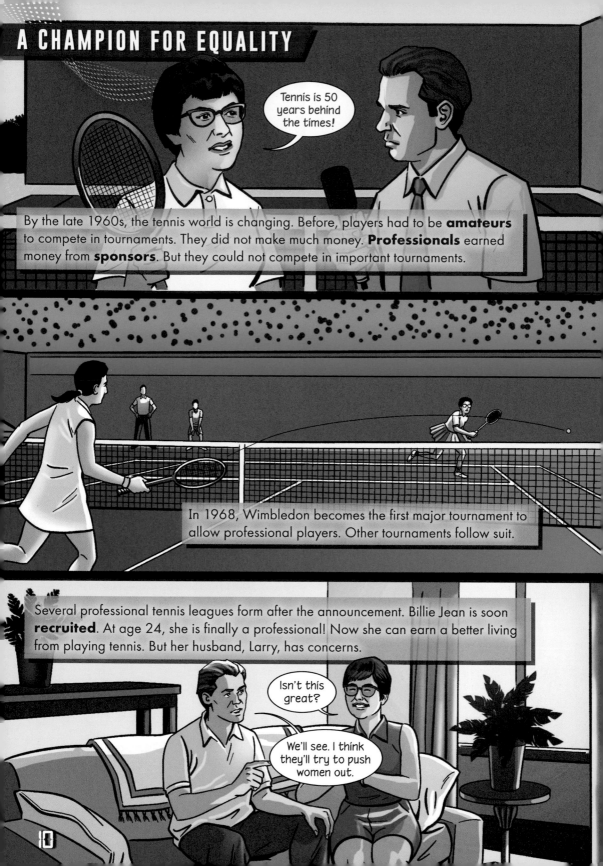

A CHAMPION FOR EQUALITY

Tennis is 50 years behind the times!

By the late 1960s, the tennis world is changing. Before, players had to be **amateurs** to compete in tournaments. They did not make much money. **Professionals** earned money from **sponsors**. But they could not compete in important tournaments.

In 1968, Wimbledon becomes the first major tournament to allow professional players. Other tournaments follow suit.

Several professional tennis leagues form after the announcement. Billie Jean is soon **recruited**. At age 24, she is finally a professional! Now she can earn a better living from playing tennis. But her husband, Larry, has concerns.

Isn't this great?

We'll see. I think they'll try to push women out.

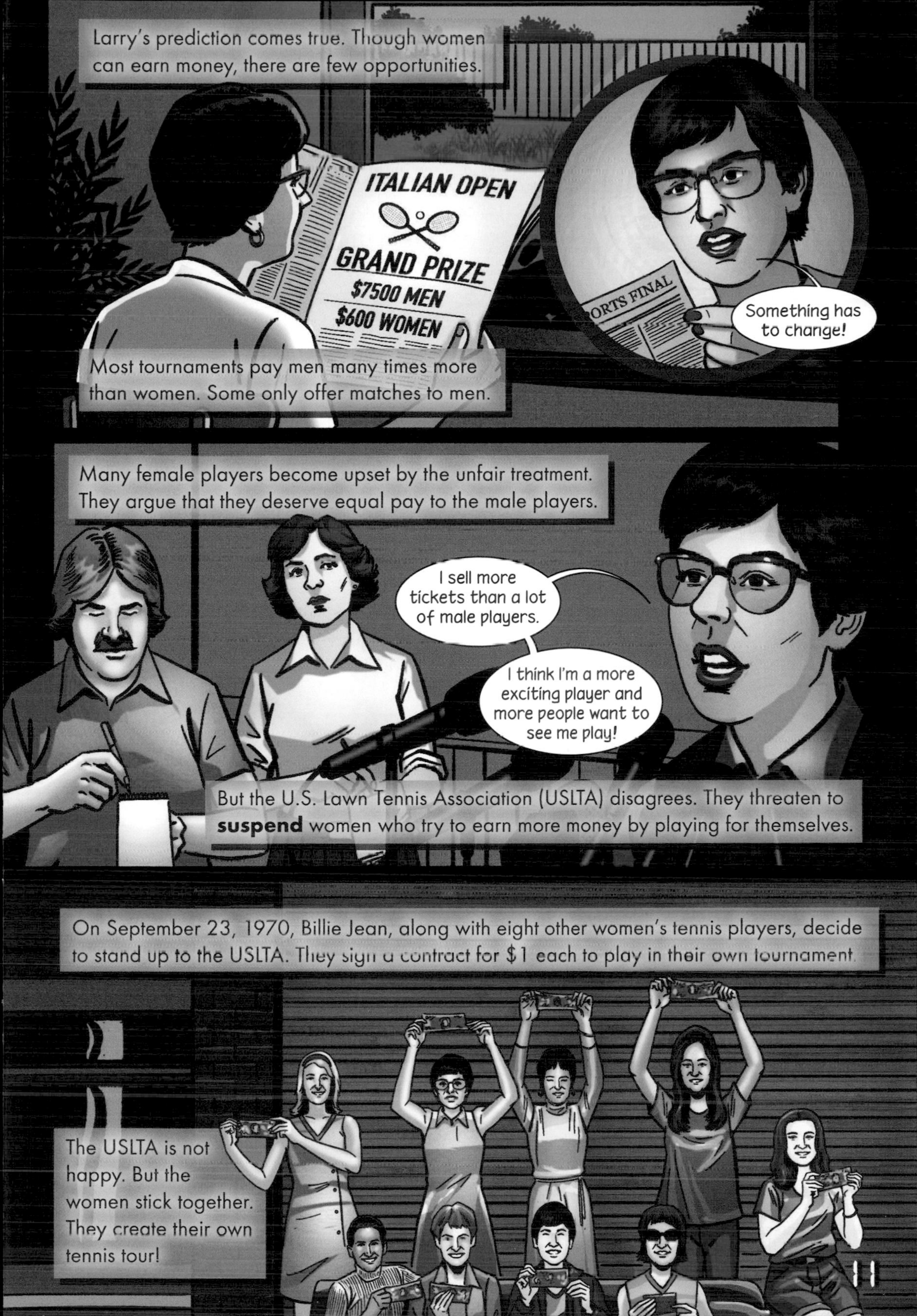
Larry's prediction comes true. Though women can earn money, there are few opportunities.
ITALIAN OPEN
GRAND PRIZE
$7500 MEN
$600 WOMEN
ORTS FINAL
Something has to change!
Most tournaments pay men many times more than women. Some only offer matches to men.
Many female players become upset by the unfair treatment. They argue that they deserve equal pay to the male players.
I sell more tickets than a lot of male players.
I think I'm a more exciting player and more people want to see me play!
But the U.S. Lawn Tennis Association (USLTA) disagrees. They threaten to **suspend** women who try to earn more money by playing for themselves.
On September 23, 1970, Billie Jean, along with eight other women's tennis players, decide to stand up to the USLTA. They sign a contract for $1 each to play in their own tournament.
The USLTA is not happy. But the women stick together. They create their own tennis tour!

The women's tour keeps the players busy. They play almost every week.

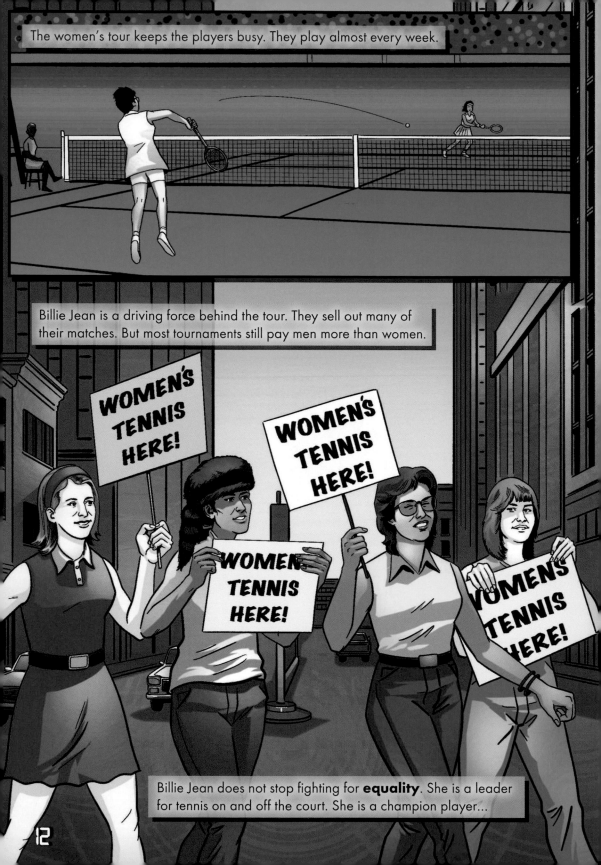

Billie Jean is a driving force behind the tour. They sell out many of their matches. But most tournaments still pay men more than women.

WOMEN'S TENNIS HERE!

WOMEN'S TENNIS HERE!

WOMEN TENNIS HERE!

WOMENS TENNIS HERE!

Billie Jean does not stop fighting for **equality**. She is a leader for tennis on and off the court. She is a champion player...

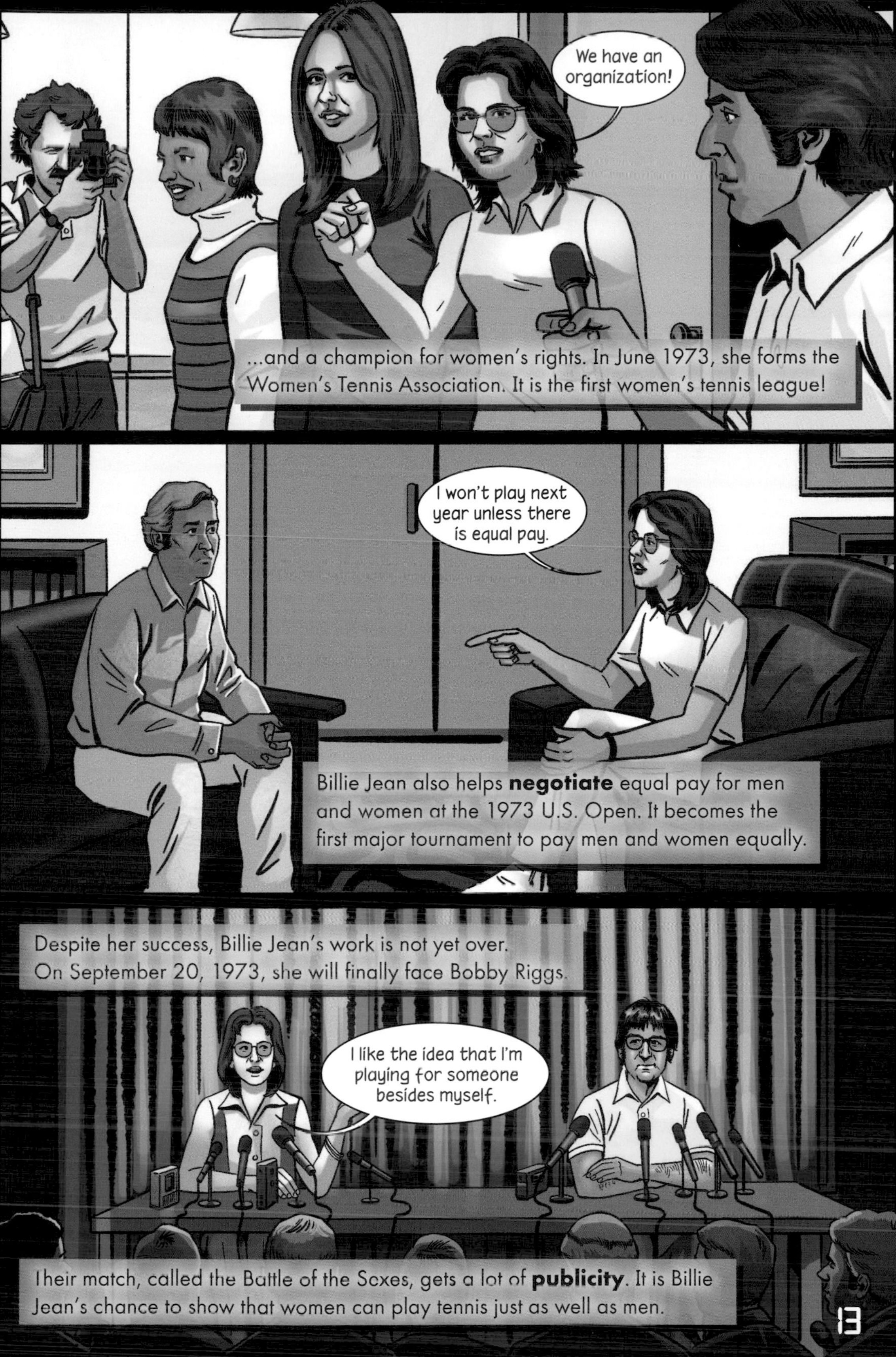
We have an organization!
...and a champion for women's rights. In June 1973, she forms the Women's Tennis Association. It is the first women's tennis league!
I won't play next year unless there is equal pay.
Billie Jean also helps **negotiate** equal pay for men and women at the 1973 U.S. Open. It becomes the first major tournament to pay men and women equally.
Despite her success, Billie Jean's work is not yet over. On September 20, 1973, she will finally face Bobby Riggs.
I like the idea that I'm playing for someone besides myself.
Their match, called the Battle of the Sexes, gets a lot of **publicity**. It is Billie Jean's chance to show that women can play tennis just as well as men.

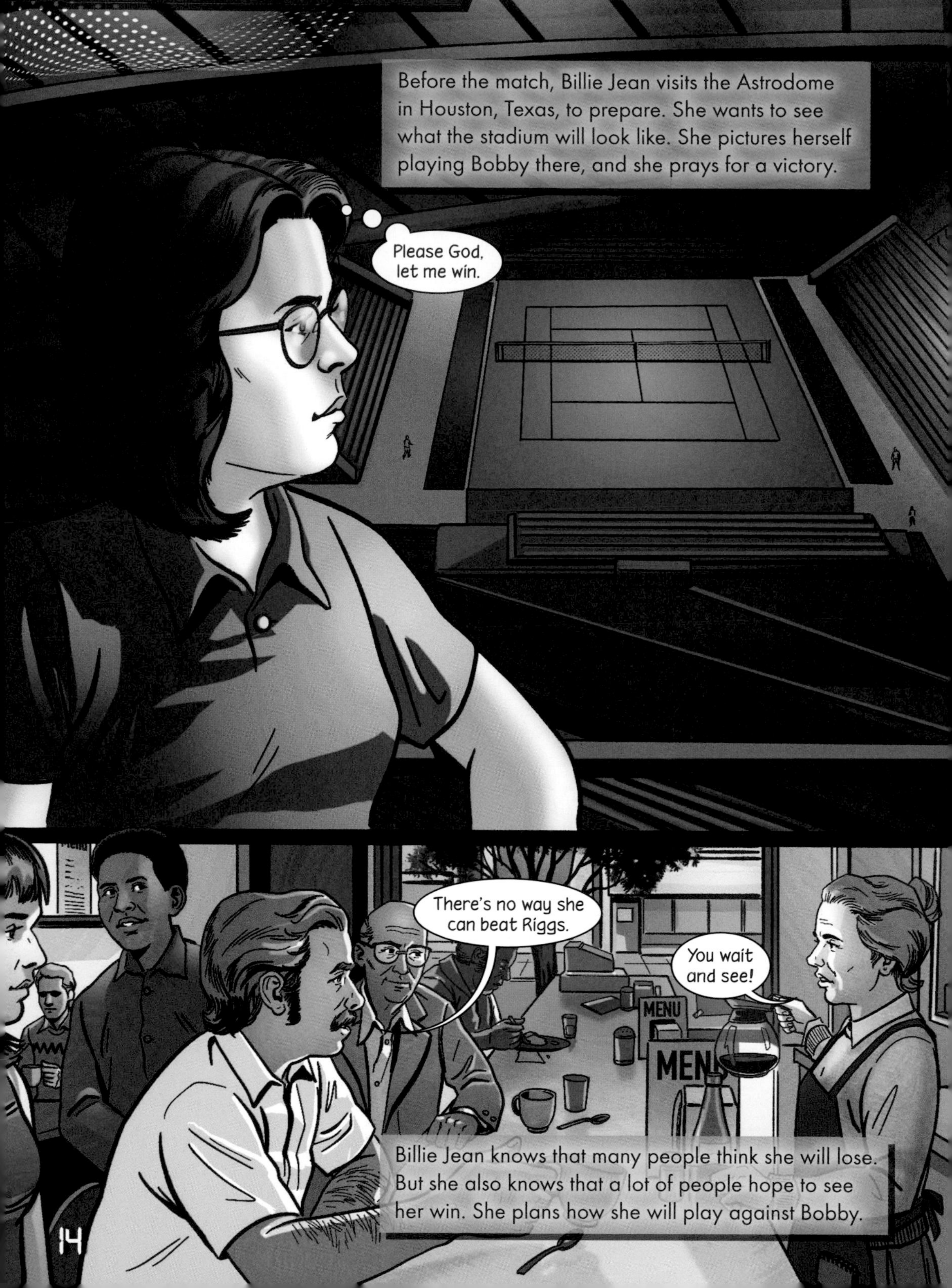
Before the match, Billie Jean visits the Astrodome in Houston, Texas, to prepare. She wants to see what the stadium will look like. She pictures herself playing Bobby there, and she prays for a victory.
Please God, let me win.
There's no way she can beat Riggs.
You wait and see!
MENU
Billie Jean knows that many people think she will lose. But she also knows that a lot of people hope to see her win. She plans how she will play against Bobby.

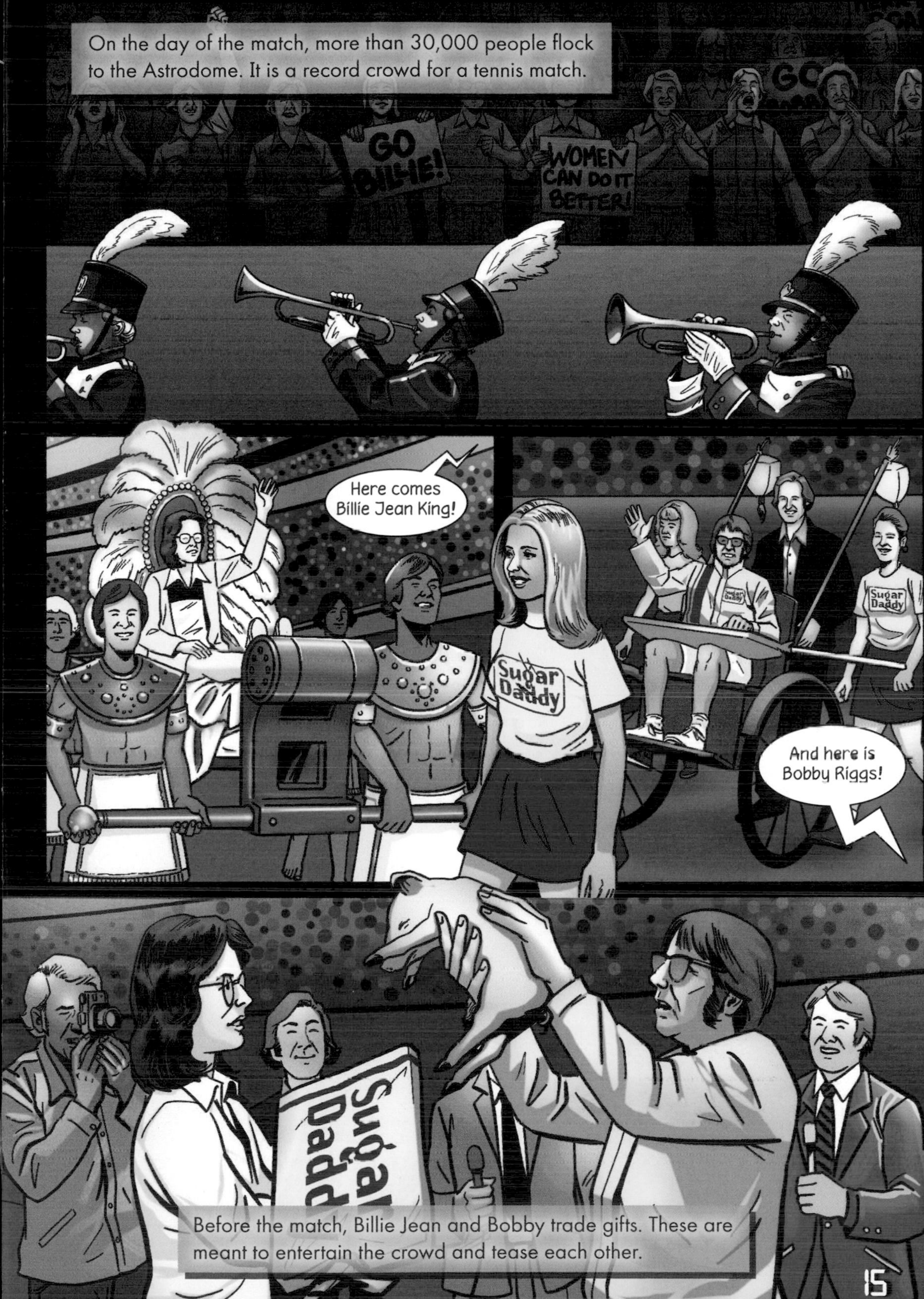
On the day of the match, more than 30,000 people flock to the Astrodome. It is a record crowd for a tennis match.
GO BILLIE!
WOMEN CAN DO IT BETTER!
Here comes Billie Jean King!
Sugar Daddy
And here is Bobby Riggs!
Before the match, Billie Jean and Bobby trade gifts. These are meant to entertain the crowd and tease each other.

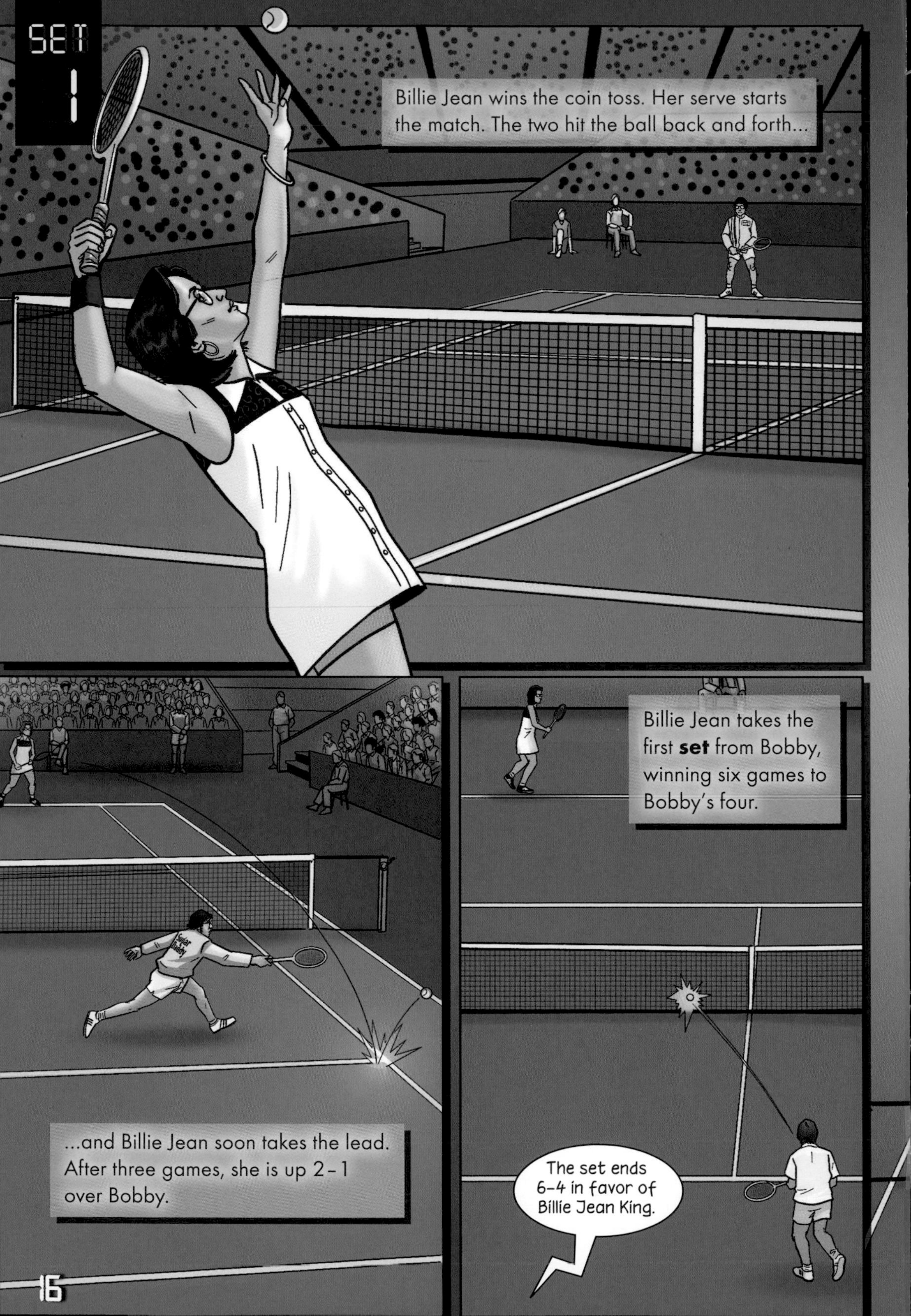
SET 1
Billie Jean wins the coin toss. Her serve starts the match. The two hit the ball back and forth...
...and Billie Jean soon takes the lead. After three games, she is up 2–1 over Bobby.
Billie Jean takes the first **set** from Bobby, winning six games to Bobby's four.
The set ends 6–4 in favor of Billie Jean King.

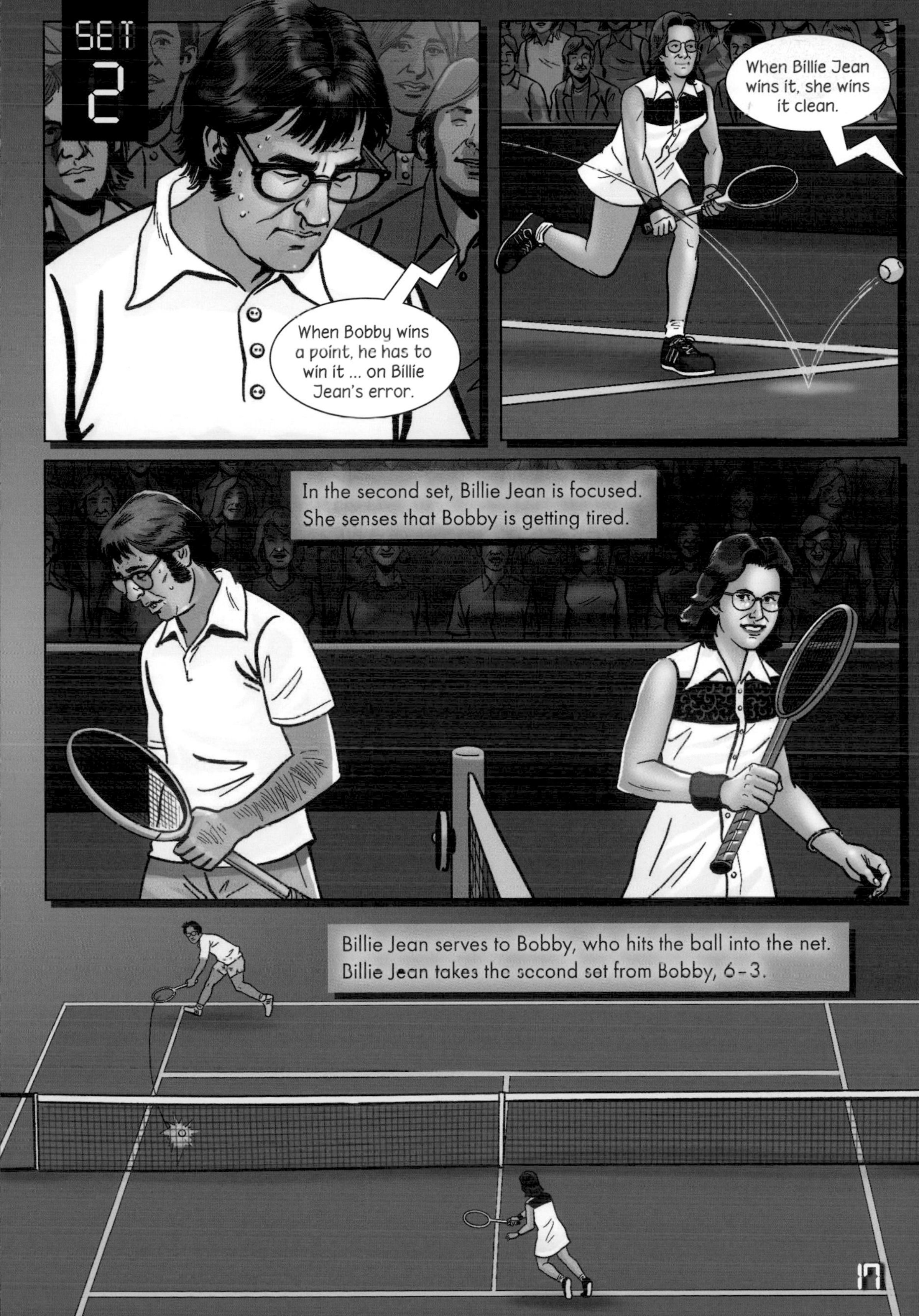
SET
2
When Bobby wins a point, he has to win it ... on Billie Jean's error.
When Billie Jean wins it, she wins it clean.
In the second set, Billie Jean is focused. She senses that Bobby is getting tired.
Billie Jean serves to Bobby, who hits the ball into the net. Billie Jean takes the second set from Bobby, 6–3.

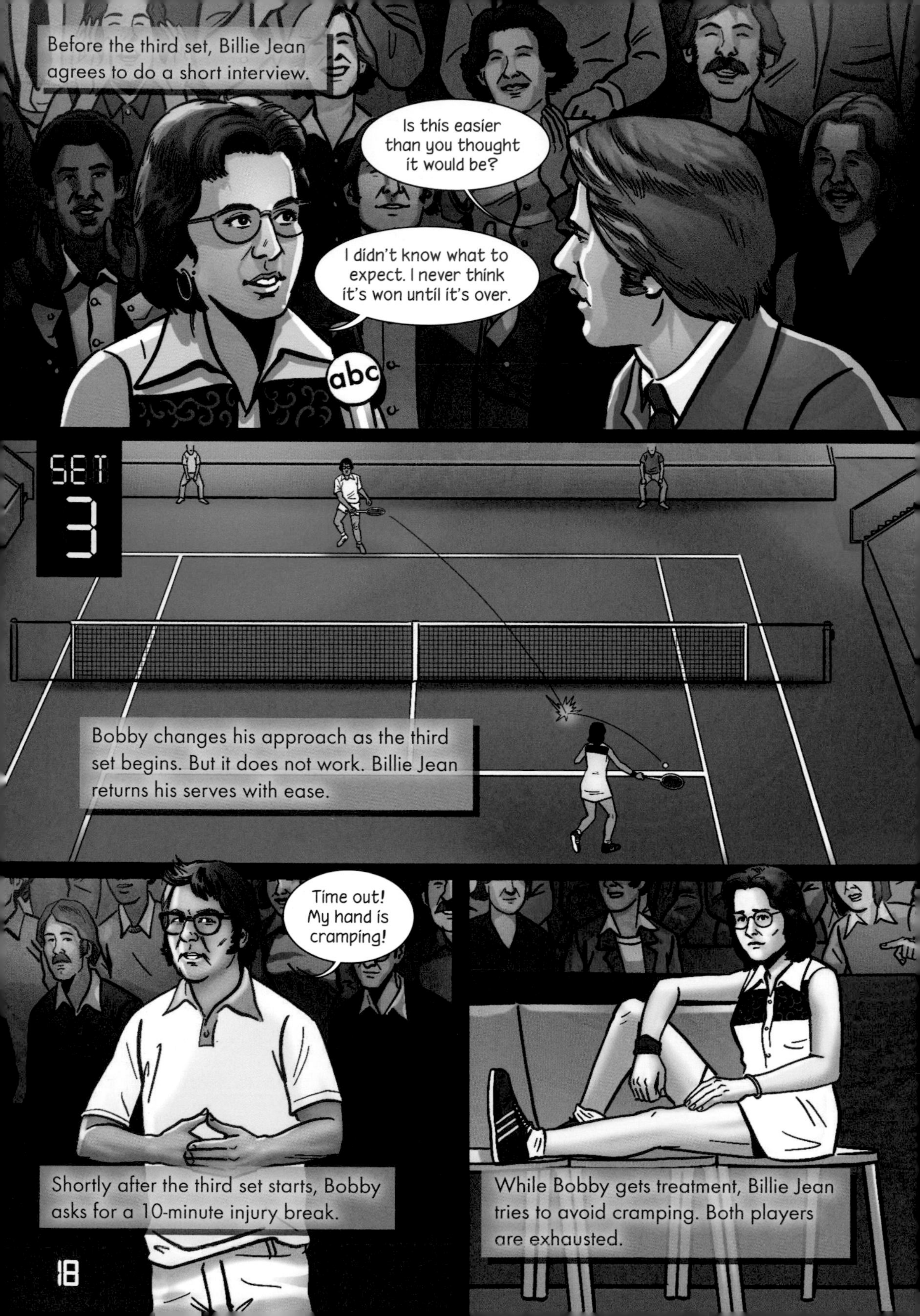
Before the third set, Billie Jean agrees to do a short interview.
Is this easier than you thought it would be?
I didn't know what to expect. I never think it's won until it's over.
abc
SET 3
Bobby changes his approach as the third set begins. But it does not work. Billie Jean returns his serves with ease.
Time out! My hand is cramping!
Shortly after the third set starts, Bobby asks for a 10-minute injury break.
While Bobby gets treatment, Billie Jean tries to avoid cramping. Both players are exhausted.

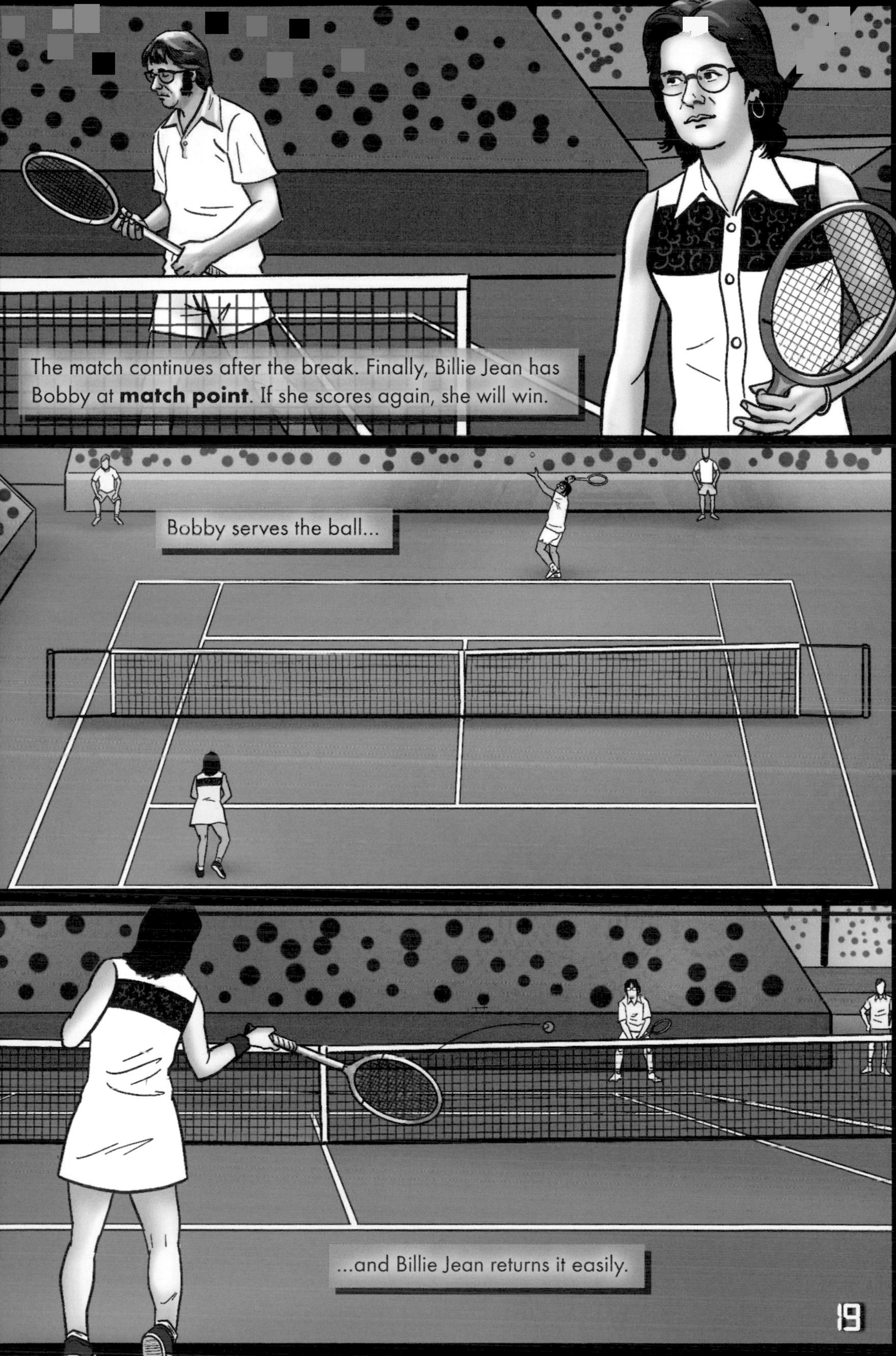
The match continues after the break. Finally, Billie Jean has Bobby at match point. If she scores again, she will win.
Bobby serves the ball...
...and Billie Jean returns it easily.

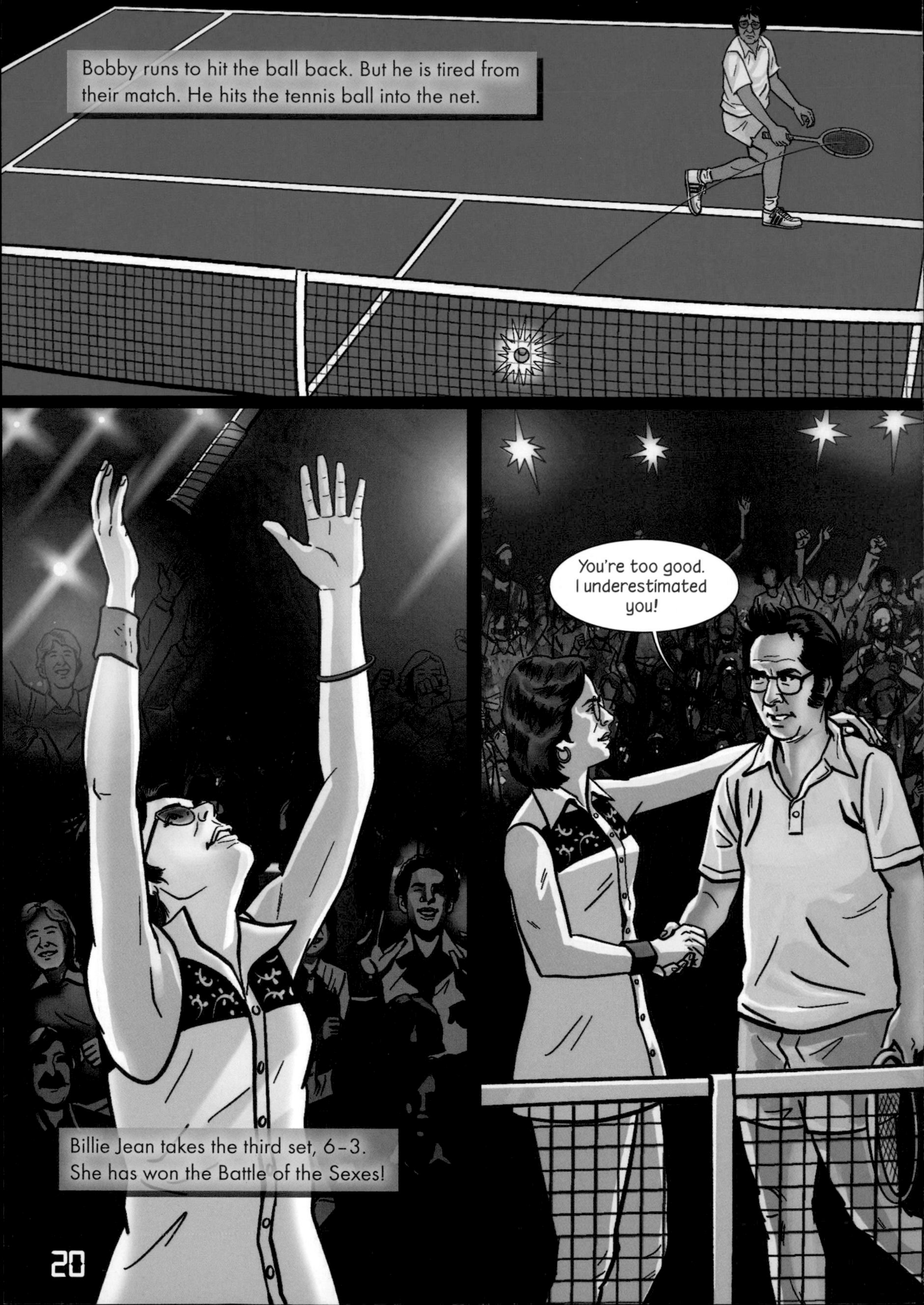
Bobby runs to hit the ball back. But he is tired from their match. He hits the tennis ball into the net.
Billie Jean takes the third set, 6–3. She has won the Battle of the Sexes!
You're too good. I underestimated you!

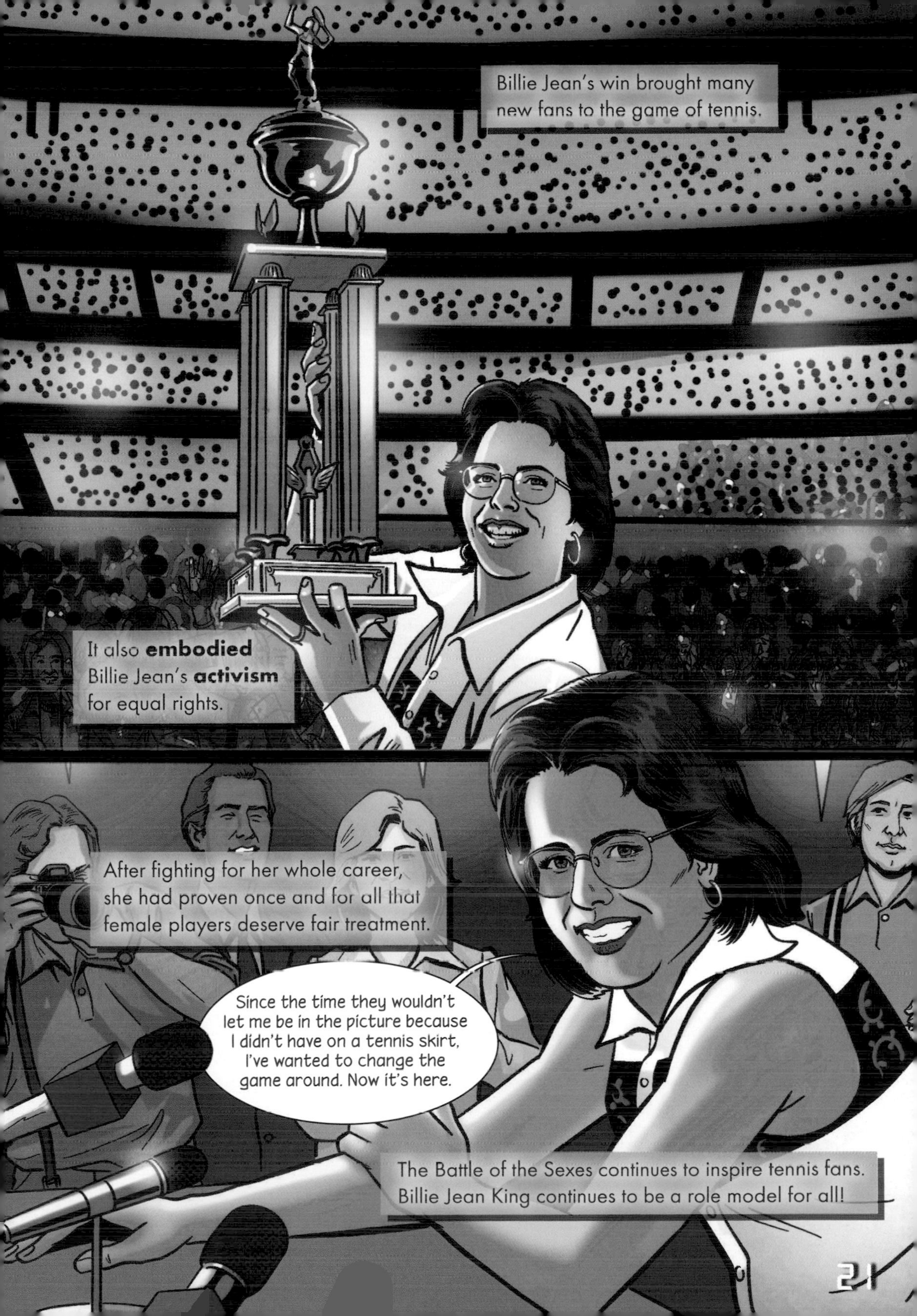
Billie Jean's win brought many new fans to the game of tennis.
It also **embodied** Billie Jean's **activism** for equal rights.
After fighting for her whole career, she had proven once and for all that female players deserve fair treatment.
Since the time they wouldn't let me be in the picture because I didn't have on a tennis skirt, I've wanted to change the game around. Now it's here.
The Battle of the Sexes continues to inspire tennis fans. Billie Jean King continues to be a role model for all!

MORE ABOUT BILLIE JEAN KING

- An audience of about 90 million people watched the Battle of the Sexes live on television.

- Throughout her career, Billie Jean King won 12 singles titles, 16 women's doubles titles, and 11 mixed doubles titles.

- Billie Jean King was inducted into the International Tennis Hall of Fame in 1987.

- Billie Jean King has also become an activist for LGBTQ+ rights.

BILLIE JEAN KING TIMELINE

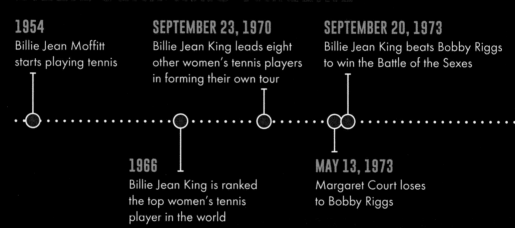

1954
Billie Jean Moffitt starts playing tennis

SEPTEMBER 23, 1970
Billie Jean King leads eight other women's tennis players in forming their own tour

SEPTEMBER 20, 1973
Billie Jean King beats Bobby Riggs to win the Battle of the Sexes

1966
Billie Jean King is ranked the top women's tennis player in the world

MAY 13, 1973
Margaret Court loses to Bobby Riggs

BILLIE JEAN KING'S BIRTHPLACE
LONG BEACH, CALIFORNIA

BATTLE OF THE SEXES MATCH
HOUSTON, TEXAS

GLOSSARY

activism—efforts made to support a certain cause

amateurs—people who are not paid for an activity

doubles—tennis matches played by two players on each team

embodied—represented an idea

equality—the state of being treated fairly or the same as others

match—a contest between two sides in tennis, usually decided by the best two-out-of-three sets for women and the best three-out-of-five sets for men

match point—a situation during a tennis match in which a player can win the match by scoring the next point

negotiate—to work out an agreement

professionals—people who are paid for an activity

publicity—attention given to someone or something by the media

recruited—tried to convince someone to join a group or activity

set—a series of games in a tennis match; a player wins a set when they win six games and have at least two more wins than their opponent.

sponsors—individuals or groups that give money to an event or person to advertise for their business or cause

suspend—to force someone to give up a position for a time

tournament—an organized series of contests in which players compete for one overall prize

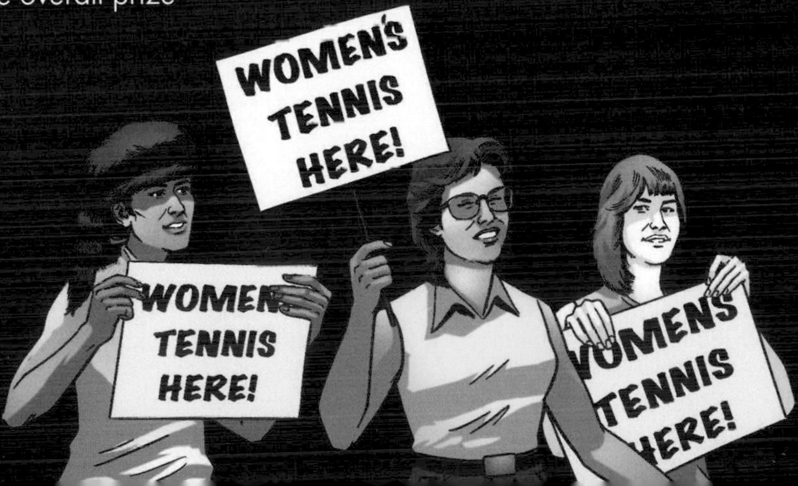

WOMEN'S TENNIS HERE!
WOMEN TENNIS HERE!
TENNIS

TO LEARN MORE

AT THE LIBRARY

Rockliff, Mara. *Billie Jean!: How Tennis Star Billie Jean King Changed Women's Sports*. New York, N.Y.: G.P. Putnam's Sons, 2019.

Skinner, J.E. *Billie Jean King vs. Bobby Riggs*. Ann Arbor, Mich.: Cherry Lake Publishing, 2019.

Terrell, Brandon. *A Win for Women: Billie Jean King Takes Down Bobby Riggs*. North Mankato, Minn.: Capstone Press, 2019.

ON THE WEB

FACTSURFER

Factsurfer.com gives you a safe, fun way to find more information.

1. Go to www.factsurfer.com
2. Enter "Billie Jean King" into the search box and click 🔍.
3. Select your book cover to see a list of related content.

INDEX